Memoirs of a School Nurse: You can't make this stuff up!

Kelly Riemenschneider

Memoirs of a School Nurse: You Can't Make This Stuff Up!

First Edition
Copyright 2013 Kelly Riemenschneider

ISBN: 978-1-304-23701-9

Dedicated to a happy life,
Laughing every day and loving your job.

Writing a book was not on my "to-do" list. Certainly, everyone dreams of being an author at one time or another. That makes this an unrealized dream come true.

I have thirty-five years experience as a nurse and caregiver to children and animals. I married my best friend 34 years ago and we are still very much in love. Our daughter Nicole is grown and married. She was a pleasure to raise, except for that one time and that other time, but all in all a pleasure. We are proud of her and her accomplishments. She is forming her own life lessons and cares about others.

I have been encouraged to write a book several times. I decided to sit down one day to put some thoughts together. The subject was always clear. As I started to write, the memories started to come back, some days in a flood of post-it notes.

I have learned a lot over the years and have found the life lessons I want to live by. I may not have always made the best choices, but I have learned something from each of my choices. I choose to find the lighter side of situations and laugh. No one's life is perfect. When things aren't going how you would like, it is your responsibility to take control and make changes to your life to make it happy and fulfilling.

I hope you will enjoy reading this as much as I have enjoyed writing it. Follow along as I deal with caring for animals, my years as a nurse, my accident-prone husband and even my own crazy accidents. You will follow my path to a new career as a school nurse. This new career gives me more than I ever thought I would be able to find in a job. I found on looking back, my whole life fits together like puzzle pieces and it all made sense. Some of the things that I have seen and heard, no one would ever believe. You just can't make this stuff up!

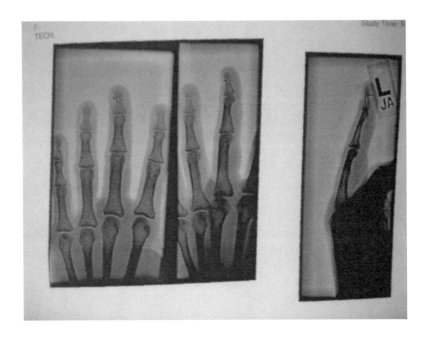

After reviewing the x-ray the diagnosis has been confirmed; you have a sewing needle in your finger.

Memoirs of a School Nurse: You Can't Make This Stuff Up!

Contents

Chapter 1: I want to be a nurse

From an early age, I knew I wanted to be a nurse. It seemed to be a sign when I got a book for my birthday from my aunt called, "A Job for Nurse Kelly". My junior and senior years of high school, I worked at the local hospital as a "student aide". I saw things I could have never imagined, helped take care of classmates injured in car accidents at prom time, passed out dinner trays and bedpans. I learned a lot and it was a great insight into being a nurse. I got accepted to the Licensed Practical Nursing program for the fall. Over the summer after graduation, I worked at one of the local nursing homes until school started. I thought the more experience in the medical profession the better.

I pretty much breezed through high school. I never had to really study. Nursing school was much different. The first day of school, we already had a test scheduled for the next day. It was a lot of memorizing and hours of studying.

I had a lot of hands on training in local hospitals, clinics and nursing homes. I liked the patient contact. I even took care of one of my parent's friends who had surgery at a hospital I had clincials at.

I worked in the Pediatric Ward in one of the hospitals. I took care of the cutest three year old. He had coffee thrown on him by his mother. I was horrified! I explained everything to him that I was doing, even when I was going to supper. He was smiley and happy despite why he was there. The second night, I told him I was going to supper and would be back in a little while. My classmates and I had missed meeting up, so I just headed down to eat. They told me they had gone to his room to see if I had left for the cafeteria. He told them, "Kewwy went to eat supper." It was the start of realizing how smart children are. They are impressionable and soak up knowledge like a sponge. I always loved kids. My brother came along when I was ten years old. I took care of him a lot. I felt comfortable with babies even back when I was ten.

I graduated the following July and was offered a job back at the hospital I had worked as a student aide. I took my boards in October and was issued my license.

I started out on the day shift during my orientation. I got put on straight nights after three months. I hated it. I never thought about having to work another shift, weekends and holidays. After a year of nights, I got back on days. I worked mostly on the Coronary Care Unit that also had general medical patients and a small pediatric unit. No one else cared much for being assigned to the little patients. I loved it, so it worked out great!

Before all the changes to healthcare, people were admitted for x-ray procedures, cataract surgery and my favorite: "We have medical assistance and want to go away for the weekend, so let's get our child admitted to the hospital." The children ranged in age from infant to three years old. They usually were sick. I would bathe them, go with them for their chest x-ray and rock them to sleep in the rocking chair. Kids aren't dumb! When mom would come to pick them up on Monday morning, they clung to me and wouldn't even look at mom. They knew they had been dumped off.

I floated to other units in the hospital and gained a lot of good experience. I was even floated to the nursery. I loved it! I became rather type A about those babies looking sharp and swaddled. I washed their hair, changed their diapers, wrapped them in a clean blanket and got them out to their mothers. They were all turned from side to side to change their position during each shift. They all faced the same way at the same time! I was young and pretty meek, except on this one day I worked in the nursery. We had a full nursery and more babies on the way. I was bathing all those babies and washing their hair. One of the regular nurses on the unit came in and told me I didn't have time to be washing their hair today! I looked at her and told her, "Don't tell me how to take care of my babies!" I wasn't even the regular nursery nurse, but I didn't care. It takes thirty seconds to wash their little heads. It was important to me that their hair smelled like baby shampoo and was combed. I thought that was how they should smell and look!

January of my senior year of high school I met the love of my life, Steve. We met through a mutual friend at the bowling alley. Isn't that romantic? He graduated from a different school the year before. From the moment we met, I knew we were meant to be together. We spent all of our free time together. He took me to my senior prom. He came to my graduation ceremony and my friend's graduation party by the lake. He fit right in and everyone liked him. He was supportive of my nursing career right from the start. We got married almost a year after I started working at the hospital.

Getting pregnant was quite a challenge for us. It only happened once. Five years later, I gave birth to our daughter Nicole. I worked up until the day before I went into labor. The delivery room nurse announced her birth over the intercom system. The patients I had taken care of the day before couldn't believe I had the baby! Nicole often came with me when I had staff meetings at the hospital. It wasn't unusual for a staff member to take her for a walk or to go find a snack. She grew up feeling comfortable in the hospital and became familiar with medical jargon. Both Steve and Nicole have gotten good at reading the notes I leave for them. They are always sprinkled with medical abbreviations. Our bedding has always had mitered corner folds and I have a nicely stocked medicine and first aid cabinet. You never know when somebody might have an accident!

I worked at the hospital for many years. We had the "regulars" who you could count on like clockwork to be admitted to the hospital. Some of those patients you couldn't help but get attached to. I took other job opportunities while I worked there. I learned how to draw blood and went to the three nursing homes in town once a week; I assisted in Risk Management, patient complaints and Infection Control. I always knew there weren't as many opportunities for LPN's. I had no real desire to go back and get my RN. Being a floor nurse was hard work and required some heavy lifting, which is not something you can do forever.

I like to give shots. I know, right? Insulin, pain shots, B12 shots, it doesn't matter. I use to do mantoux tests and flu shots. A co-worker told me one time that I was brutal with giving shots! Let me tell you, pushing a needle in slowly hurts way more than doing it quickly to get it over with. I like drawing blood, too. I like to use what they call a "butterfly" needle. The needle is small and works great for patients that are hard to find a vein to draw blood from. My learning to draw blood consisted of reading a booklet one night and practicing on the lab manager the next day. No pressure! I had one patient that was tough to draw. I couldn't see any veins to use. An old pro told me he had drawn the patient the day before; just use the same spot. That was literally blind faith, but I did as he said and got my blood sample!

We always did a lot of things with our daughter Nicole as she was growing up. I cut back from full time to three days a week after she was born. I worked my vacations around her days off from school, so we could do things together. We always thought it was important to help her learn and show her how to explore the world. Steve and I tried to find a balance between enough family time and letting her do independent activities. It would be easy to smother her since she is an only child. We helped her friends out when they needed help and got along well with them. Our lives pretty much revolved around her.

I made a move over to the hospital's homecare/hospice department after more than twenty years. It was a big change. I scheduled staff visits, worked with insurance companies and took doctor's orders. I didn't have to wear a uniform. I didn't do patient care any more.

Nicole was about to start at an art college in a few weeks. She had gone to test for her black belt in karate. She earned her black belt, but came home with a sore ankle. It then became both ankles that were sore and swollen. After many doctor's visits and tests, she was found to have an autoimmune disorder that affects the joints much as rheumatoid arthritis does. Her ankles and wrists were so swollen. She wanted to start college. We were afraid she would be more depressed than she already was, if she couldn't start. I got the ok to help her at school. I drove her each day and sat in on her classes to take notes for her, picked up supplies and assisted with assignments for the first two weeks of school. After adjusting and changing medications, she got better and stabilized so she could go to college independently. Doing art was hard on her wrists, so wisely she switched schools to add another major. She graduated with a double major. She does artwork on the side and has a fulfilling career as well.

The homecare job changed and grew as time went by. My days got busier and more stressful. I had trouble getting lunch breaks and getting out of work on time. I was on the phone a lot. I was good at my job, having a lot of knowledge and experience. Nicole graduated from college, moved out and settled into a townhome. Steve and I didn't need our lives to revolve around Nicole any more. I decided we needed to get a new hobby.

I thought it would be fun to get a motorcycle. The minute Steve heard those words come out of my mouth; we were on our way out the door to the

Harley shop! He was afraid I would change my mind. We bought a nice

smaller size Harley. We got our permits to drive then went to motorcycle

safety classes. He got through it. I didn't. I have "can't drive a clutch"

deficit. I tried, really I did. The instructors couldn't believe I came back the

second day. I was so unnerved by it, that I quit. I was mad at myself and

disappointed. I rode on the back of the motorcycle with Steve. It was fun!

The next year when our anniversary came around, Steve had decided to buy

me a special present. He bought me a motorcycle! I had seen a motorcycle

brand on-line that was small, lightweight and an automatic. I was excited

and scared to death. Dang, now I really have to learn how to ride this and get

my license! I only dumped it once! We rode together over the summer. I got

comfortable and gained experience over the next couple of months. I set up

an appointment to take my test with the DMV the end of August. I was

nervous. There are three people that do testing at the DMV. Two of them

intimidated me; the other one was very nice. When I found out who was the

one doing my test, my anxiety level went way down! I passed my test and

got my motorcycle endorsement. Yay!

The job in homecare kept getting more stressful. I cried and was upset

more than not. I started casually looking to go back to the hospital or find a new job. The economy went bad and there were no jobs to be found. I am not a risk taker. I would never quit a job without having a new one.

Chapter 2: My accident-prone husband

Early on in our relationship, I could see that Steve was accident-prone. Being a nurse was a bonus for him. I don't know if that was on his wish list when looking for a girlfriend/wife, but for him, it was a good idea!

While in college, he worked at a liquor store as a cashier/manager. Before the days of self-serve, liquor stores had high school boys they hired as "carry-outs". They got the beer from the cooler and of course carried out purchases for customers. One night, a customer wanted a bag of ice. The carryout went in the cooler to get it. Boys being boys, it was common to toss it to a customer. This time, Steve was in the middle and got beaned in the head with a 20-pound bag of ice. He spent the night in the hospital under observation for a possible concussion.

Things that an accident-prone person shouldn't do, like woodworking and fishing for example, he enjoys. I use to go fishing with him. I was in love and we were together. It was so boring! The only thing good about it was getting a tan! He brought three or four fishing rods. He would cast each rod until it got hung up on something. When all the rods were snagged, he would slowly work at getting each one unsnagged. It drove me crazy!

He has become really good at woodworking over the years, but it does come with pains. He has routered his finger, sanded a nail or two and my favorite: hit his finger with the hammer. How do you even keep a straight face when he tells you that?

One time when I worked at the hospital and Nicole was three, he was going to work on our back deck. I worked every other weekend on the day shift. I went to take a break in the cafeteria that Saturday morning. The next thing I know, a co-worker is carrying Nicole in to the cafeteria. I am puzzled how she got there and where are her shoes? While working on the deck, he had slipped with the wonder bar and cut his leg above the knee pretty deep. He knew enough to put pressure on the wound. He found an ace wrap and wrapped it around his knee. He grabbed Nicole and got in his truck and drove to the hospital. He recognized one of the doctors in the parking lot. He handed Nicole over to him and headed down to the ER. That's when Nicole was taken down to the nursing station I worked on and handed over to a co-worker. I grabbed Nicole and went into the ER to see what had happened. Steve didn't have any shoes on either! He got his cut stitched up and drove back home with Nicole.

I had just had gallbladder surgery about a week before. Steve and Nicole are out in the front yard playing catch with the ball. She was twelve. I am relaxing, reading a book. Nicole comes in the house, "Mom?" "Mom?" I answer back. She asks me if I would come outside and see dad. "I am good here, Nicole." Again, she calmly asks, "Can you come outside and see dad?"

"I am reading Nicole." This time she decided to elaborate a bit more, "Dad is hurt, can you come outside?" I am out the door in an instant and there across the lawn I see him laying face first next to our ravine that is lined with rock. He isn't saying a word. I stood there, stunned. "Steve?" "Yeah?" "Are you okay?" "I think so." Here comes my line that I say from here on out: "What did you do now?" "I was playing catch with Nicole. She threw the ball high, I tried to catch it and fell into the ravine." I walked over and helped him sit up. Blooding was trickling down his face. Facial cuts bleed a lot. His hands were full of blood. "We are going to the ER." (another line I have said several times) Being type A, I wasn't going to just let him in my car and get blood all over! I took him over to the faucet, washed the blood off, and gave him a clean towel. Of course, I knew the ER doctor. He teasingly asked me if I took a rolling pin to Steve's head! He got stitched up and I took him home.

Over the years, he has gotten more and more into fishing. He got a fishing kayak a few years ago. He loves to look at lures. Bores me to death! One time we went to Bass Pro Shop in Fort Myers and I sat in a rocking chair and talked on my cell phone until he was done. I have teased him more than once about coming back tomorrow and picking him up when he is done looking.

Speaking of fishing lures. I always tell him he has to wear a life jacket or he's not going fishing. In the summer, he gets up early on Saturdays and goes fishing at a local lake. He always comes home around 9am. Unless, the fish aren't biting or they are biting or he's had an accident. Lucky for me, or lucky for him (if he wants to keep fishing) it doesn't happen very often.

It was twice in one summer! The first time, it was a really nice lure to the finger. He tried to get it out himself and a boat came speeding by and swamped him. What a site! He is soaking wet, full of mud and has a fishing lure with multiple hooks stuck in his finger. He is cold. I help him out of the wet clothes and mud filled shoes. Being type A- he needs to shower first to clean up and get the lake water off. We get to the ER and this doctor is a fisherman. He wants to know what kind of lure it is, how it is to use a kayak fishing, how were the fish biting. The lure was too good to just cut it up, so the doctor saves the lure and Steve's hand looks awful! His hand was bandaged up and I take him home. The best part was the next day when he went back to look for fishing tackle and supplies he lost when he got swamped.

The second time, he was wrestling with a fish that decided to dive under the kayak. Steve leaned and over he went into the lake. It was late in the season, so the water was really cold. "Oh, he's home earlier than 9am, what did he do this time?" He was soaking wet, full of mud and freezing. I helped him get his clothes off; he got in the shower and then went to bed. That was the end of late season fishing!

Then there was the time he took our 35-pound sheltie for a walk before work. This morning Steve wasn't paying attention. Cody saw something and took off in another direction, pulling Steve off his feet. He did a face plant into the pavement. He had a horrible case of road rash and no honorable war story to tell. I told him, "At least it wasn't a 5-pound dog! I would tell people the dog was over 100-pounds!"

Steve got up about 4am to go to the bathroom. The way he was laying in bed, his foot had fallen asleep. He got up and did an immediate drop and roll. He assured me he was fine and went to work. A couple of hours later he was at the clinic. An x-ray showed he had broken a bone in his foot. This was two weeks after I had a tendon release in my left elbow. We looked like we'd been in a train wreck at our house.

You just can't make this stuff up! Just last week, we redid our front entryway. Steve was putting the wood trim back. He had that look on his face. "What did you do now?" "Put a nail hole in my finger." He knows the drill, put pressure on it and I fix it up!

Chapter 3: We were meant to be together

To be fair, I have had my fair share of accidents over the years. There was the day I went with my dad to get some sod. I was maybe four. I got in his truck and he shut the door for me. Doo-da-doo! I'm sitting there ready to go and dad gets in on the driver's side. He takes one look at me; gets out and opens the passenger door. My thumb was in the door. Geez, that hurt, but then I couldn't go with to get sod.

In kindergarten, we had a small wheelbarrow in the classroom to play with. Thinking about it now, who does that? A boy was pushing me around in the wheelbarrow. When the teacher announced playtime was over, he dropped the wheelbarrow with me in it and took off. The wheelbarrow landed on two of my fingers and I needed stiches. Dumb boy!

There was the time that I was out in my grandparents pasture with my dad. He was putting up new fencing. He was pulling up the old barbed wire, some of which was down, so it needed to be pulled out of the grass and dirt. For the life of me I don't know what as a six year old I could have been doing to help. All I know is, I got in the middle of my dad and some barbed wire he was pulling. When it broke loose, I was in its path and it pulled me off my feet. Oh, nasty cut! I am NOT going to let you take me for stiches like the wheelbarrow incident. That was awful! They stuck a needle in my cut and used a needle to sew it up. I wouldn't hold still, so they took my pillow away. My mom didn't feel so good and they had her put her head between her knees. I have a nice battle scar on my knee, but no stiches!

My type A personality was coming out even in elementary school. I am sitting on the back deck. Doo-da-doo! This deck is dirty, I am going to wipe it off with my hand and get a big old sliver all the way across my palm. "MOM!" She got it out, but I don't know how. I couldn't look; it hurt!

When Nicole was a baby, she accidently hit me square in the mouth with the bottom of her baby bottle. My bottom front tooth was broken off. That hurt and I felt like a hillbilly "whiff a missin' tooff!"

This was so embarrassing! I fell off the bottom step of a stepladder one evening and broke a bone in my foot. I can't even tell you the number of times I have stood on the top of the ladder and never got hurt or jumped to the ground when the ladder fell over. You know that step, the one that says, "DANGER! DO NOT STAND ON THIS STEP!"

Oh the tendon surgery? Well, again no glamorous story to tell. I had tendonitis for almost two years on and off. I had conservative treatment. I had cortisone injections. I flunked out of physical therapy. Every time I would get asked if I played tennis, " No, mumble, mumble." "What?" "I did it blowing leaves out of the driveway with a leaf blower, OK?" Before I had surgery, the surgeon needed to check to make sure I didn't have nerve damage. If there was damage to nerves it meant a little more complex surgery. To check for nerve damage, he injected Novocain into my elbow and told me to come back in an hour. If my elbow still hurt after the injection, there is nerve damage. I decided to drive over to a local store and get some vacuum cleaner bags. I had no idea that my hand and arm would become completely numb and dead weight. Driving was interesting! I couldn't hold my arm up or put my hand on the steering wheel. I suddenly knew how a patient who has had a stroke felt. Of course, I am left-handed and it was my left arm. I was glad I had cash on me because I couldn't write out a check. It was the craziest thing and I could not wait for the Novocain to wear off. Thankfully, there was no pain, no nerve damage.

We are on the beach on Sanibel Island in Florida for spring break. Nicole is with us. We are enjoying the sun, the sand and looking for shells. I am walking along and hear a crunch. What was that? I cut the bottom of my foot open on a shell. It's bleeding; we are on the beach. We head back to the condo. We have no first-aid supplies. Steve goes to the grocery store and comes back with Band-Aids and Mecuricome Iodine. "Geez, why did you get that? I didn't think they even made that any more!" Steve explains we need to disinfect the cut. "Really, with that? That's gonna hurt like hell!"

Oh, boy did that sting, but I didn't get stiches! I had to wear flip-flops for a few days at work after vacation until my foot was healed. A co-worker just laughed, "That's the rich man's accident!"

Nicole moved into her new place. Steve and I helped her a lot with the inside. She wanted some sheer curtains for the full-length window next to the front door. She picked out the fabric and I brought it home to sew. It was going to be quick and easy. It was slippery and I got so involved pushing the fabric through, that my finger got in the way of the needle. It happened so fast I didn't even feel it. I just saw the needle was broke. I looked for the needle. Oh, I found it! It went through the back of my finger and was sitting behind the fingernail. I told Steve we needed to go to the ER. The nurse and x-ray technician were grossed out. Really? It was throbbing by now. The ER doctor shot my finger full of Novocain. Once he looked at the x-ray and saw that it hadn't hit the bone, he took the needle out. My finger was numb for two days, so it never hurt. It was just not very functional. I remember my grandma telling me that when she was young she had put a sewing machine needle into her finger. That will never happen to me!

We all snore; to be honest it's not attractive. I have had allergies for years so; some nights it is more of a wheeze. Steve snores; our cat Maddie purr-snores. One night, I hear snoring. I nudge Steve to knock it off. A little while later, he hears snoring and nudges me to stop. A little while later we were both awake, looking at each other and we both hear snoring. It was only then that we realized our five month old puppy Oliver who was sleeping between us, was snoring. We both started laughing. He is definitely part of this family!

Two weeks ago I was cleaning house and my hands were full of cleaning supplies. The can of window cleaner slipped out of my arms and landed square on my big toe causing a pressure laceration. I sat on the bathroom floor with pressure on it. I thought I broke it at first. I called Steve to bring me an ice pack. I felt nauseated, like I was going to pass out. I am fine! I don't need stiches. The next night, I admitted I should have had stiches.

To whatever extent Nicole wants to admit it, she's had some accidents as well. The only thing I can tell you is if you never do anything in life, you could still get hurt in a tornado or car accident. You can't live your life in a box. The more things you do, the more your odds increase that you will have an accident, you'll find a new friend or find money on the ground. Hey, $20.00!

Chapter 4: My nursing goes beyond people

I love animals and grew up with dogs, horses and cats. I did obedience training with two dogs for 4-H. I trim my own dog's hair and nails. We had horses when I was growing up. You know how animals will make a liar out of you? We had a mare that was due to foal any day. My parents had to run an errand. I was in high school. They told me, "You'll be fine! She probably won't foal while we are gone." I swear they barely got out of the driveway! The mare lies down and her water breaks. She delivered the foal just fine, but I had to break the amniotic sac and pull it off. Congratulations, it's a filly!

There was another time my parents were gone and I was home alone. I looked out the window and one of our horses had both feet in a woven wire gate. What a great, sensible horse. She stood still while I was able to get the gate in a position for her to get out of the fence.

I have taken care of pet birds and baby ducklings, messy, messy! I have even taken care of rabbits. I had to take one to the vet due to a mattery eye. I felt kind of silly sitting there, but I didn't want anything to happen to him. Have you ever given a bunny eye drops?

When we were first married, we started housesitting for people. We took care of kids, dogs, cats, horses, and even a couple cows. The kids were always fine, just busy. The animals were sometimes in need of a little extra care. Giving medications was not unusual. I have given antibiotic shots to horses. It is not much different than a human, except, you give it in their neck, they have a coat and tough skin to get through and if they decide not to cooperate, there is nothing you can do about it!

We have had two dogs and one cat in the past. Sampson was a full size collie and a year old when we got him. He was awesome! He was protective of our place and Nicole. He always barked for a reason. He woke us up one night due to a car that was in our ditch on fire! He got bit by the neighbor's dog one time because he was protecting Nicole. He grew old and was good enough to let me know when it was time to help him go to his next life. It took me two years to get over losing him.

I drove all the way to the other side of Green Bay, Wisconsin to get our second dog. Cody was a beautiful sheltie. He was a year old. He was shy and followed me around all the time. As he came out of his shell, he showed us that he had a sense of humor. He would see Steve at the kitchen sink washing dishes and quietly walk up and poke him in the back of the knee with his nose. Steve's knee would buckle. You could almost see Cody laughing. When Nicole would leave for school or work, he would sneak behind her, as she was getting ready to leave and nip her in the butt with his little front teeth. She would get so mad at him. He would quickly run up the stairs and turn to face her like he couldn't have done it!

We were so heartbroken when he was diagnosed with Lymphoma when he was ten. We chose not to put him through chemotherapy. He would be sad to be away from us once a week and I didn't want him to be miserable. The outcome would still be the same in the end. We chose to do what they call "Palliative Care". We gave him Prednisone to keep him comfortable. He loved people food. We took him for a big adventure one Saturday in Steve's truck and let him have ice cream, and French fries. He got diarrhea, but I didn't care. He had a great day. He lasted six weeks and then he stopped eating, drinking and wouldn't walk. I knew it was time. Steve and I were devastated. We lost a family member.

When Nicole was ten we got her a kitten. Don't be fooled by the sign "FREE KITTENS". They usually cost you a fortune. Jasmine was all of 5 pounds. She was born in a barn and would not use the litter box at first. She could jump high and far and we never knew where we would find her curled up sleeping. She got herself caught in the blind cords one morning before school and got the cord wrapped around her neck. Nicole was home alone and cut the cord to get her out. We took her to the vet when I got home from work. We thought she was ok other than some cuts on her paw. In the months that followed, she started having seizures. I gave her medication for years, but those medications can cause liver and kidney failure. We paid the money to have lab work done to know just what was going on. She was in liver and kidney failure. We had her put to sleep. While I am glad for this option for animals, it is never easy.

We have a second free kitty that we had gotten. Madison (Maddie) came from my parent's stray pregnant cat that showed up and adopted them. She gave birth to five kittens. A car hit her when her kittens were five weeks old and died two days later. They all needed to be bottle fed and then weaned off milk. We started them on solids and taught them how to use the litter box. Maddie is a big pretty cat with blue eyes, who acts like a dog and is very vocal. We love her!

After Cody our sheltie passed away, it was so quiet in the house. He had been an indoor dog. By a stroke of timing, Oliver came into our life. I had dog-sat Cavalier King Charles Spaniels before and just loved them in every way. I found a breeder who had one of the puppies from a recent litter come back. The buyer found a puppy to be too much work. Oliver was 3 ½ months old. We drove over to see him. They offered to let us take him outside or play with him. Steve told her there was no need, "I already know he is coming home with us!" Smart, cuddly, already potty trained and leash broke! He is a real cutie! He is twenty pounds of fun and frolic. He goes with us in the car or truck as often as we will let him. He goes with us on the airplane when we travel on vacation. He attracts a lot of attention and loves everyone!

I started doing some dog/housesitting again. Steve stays home with our pets. I move in and take care of friend's animals and their house while they go on vacation. I have taken care of older dogs. They couldn't hear, needed medications and one had lost use of her hind legs and was in a wheelchair. It made her more mobile and she got around just fine!

I stayed at a co-worker's house a couple of times. She had an older dog that was deaf and a cat that never came out to strangers. She told me I would not see Georgia the whole time I stayed. The very first night, I was sitting on the couch with the dog and out of the corner of my eye I see Georgia sneaking up to me. She jumped on the couch and into my lap! Pets will make a liar out of you every time!

Just like my patients at the hospital, you can't help but get attached. They are like extensions of my family. I took care of one dog, Duffy for several years. We are talking 3-4 weeks every January, as well as other times during the year. We had a routine and it just picked up where we left off the next time we saw each other. He slept with me on the bed at night.

Toward the end of his life, he developed congestive heart failure, and later kidney failure. The treatment for each is the opposite. The last time I took care of him, I gave him IV fluids, hand fed him and took him into the vet for follow up. I listened to his lungs and kept him comfortable. I felt like I was doing hospice care. It was the last time we would spend together. I said good-bye to him and cried like he was my own dog.

They have a new dog now, but it takes a while to get to a place where you are ready to do that. I took care of their new dog and their daughter/son-in-law's three dogs last summer. It sounds hectic, but it was fun! It was over July 4th, so I bought some red, white and blue ribbon and put on each of their collars. It was like they knew. Each dog would take his or her turn having me tie a ribbon on!

My friend has a Weimaraner named Britta. I have known her since she was a puppy. She is a big loving bundle of energy. Her only issue is separation anxiety, big time! One time she went into their downstairs bathroom and accidently closed the door on herself while they were at work. She was in such a panic to get out; she clawed deep grooves into the door. When I dog sit having a routine is key. She is fine when I take care of her and am gone at work during the day. She is not okay if I go somewhere after I come home from work. There is (was) a chair that she likes to lay on.

When she gets anxious, she starts ripping the fabric. I stitched the chair cushion back up a couple of times. Last fall, I had to go to a class after I came home from work. I came home to find the chair ripped open and a bunch of it's stuffing all over the floor. She couldn't have gotten her body any lower to the floor. She knew she messed up. I whispered, "What did you do?" She was so sad; I thought she was going to cry tears. I told her not to worry I'd fix it. I put the stuffing back in the chair and started hand sewing the fabric back in place the best I could. The whole time she was sitting behind me with her head positioned so she could look over my shoulder. A couple days later, I had to run home for a minute after I had come home from work. When I came back, the chair was ripped up to the point of no return. It was down to the wire springs! I had four-grocery bags worth of stuffing. I found a canvas drop cloth to cover the seat of the chair with and secured it in place. She still wanted to lie on her chair. It thankfully wasn't a new chair. They weren't totally surprised.

Late winter when I was getting ready for work one morning, I saw something sitting on our fence in the backyard. We have a small backyard that edges right into the woods. It was a little dark yet; I just wasn't sure what it was. I walked outside and around to the backyard. I walked up the stone steps and walked until I was two feet away from it. It was an owl! He had his eyes closed and was maybe 8-10 inches tall. I went back in and got my camera; I took a couple of pictures while I was standing right next to him. I was late leaving for work; I needed to get going. I came home and he was still perched on the fence. I knew that something wasn't right. I called the Raptor Center and they agreed. They wanted me to send them a picture to identify him and then they wanted me to try to catch him to bring him in for care. I sent the picture and he was identified as an Eastern Screech Owl. He was beautiful with black, gray and white feathers. They walked me through how to catch him. I got about five feet from him and he flew up on the roof, then he flew into a tree branch. He hung around all night and was gone the next morning. We never saw him again. We are hoping that he just ate something that didn't agree with him.

We live in the woods, only a few miles from a state park. Over the past several years, the black bear population has grown. Every year about the beginning of May, I tell Steve we need to start taking the bird feeders down at night before the bear starts coming through. A bear bends a Shepard's hooks like a piece of wire and twists the bird feeders, sometimes beyond repair. My "bearometer" kicked in the night before last and I told Steve we better start bringing in the bird feeders at night. Every year is the same, Steve nods in agreement and the next morning the bear has visited. He visited last night. I told you so.

Chapter 5: Something's missing

I was starting to get really negative. I hated my job. I couldn't find a

new one. I was afraid this was my true personality. I applied for several jobs

and didn't even get so much as an acknowledgement that they received my

résumé. I checked on-line every day for any jobs that I would like and

weren't too far to drive. My old risk management job at the hospital was

posted. I didn't even qualify for it anymore. I had the experience, but they

wanted an RN now.

I felt like something was missing in my life. Nicole was grown and

had moved out to start her own life. Don't get me wrong, it was time for her

to move out or we might pull each other's hair out! I love kids and missed

being around them. I missed doing direct patient care.

One Saturday night toward the end of August, when I was looking on-

line at job postings, I saw one for a school nurse. I had always thought I

would love to do that! Miss Negativity went back and forth about filling out

the application. I probably won't get the job; it's probably not worth filling

it out. Sunday, I went back, filled out the application and hit the send button.

Monday by mid-morning, I had a message from one of the Licensed

School Nurse supervisors that she wanted to set me up for an interview. I

had an early morning interview. I got dressed up and had permission from homecare to go to an "appointment" that morning. I would just make the time up in the workday. I got to the interview and met the supervisor. Even on the phone, I felt like I had always known her. Six or seven people interviewed me in a conference room. The position was for a school nurse at an elementary school. I was surprised that I really wasn't nervous. She walked me out, shook my hand and told me I did a great job. I left and headed back to work for the day. A co-worker asked me later in the day if I was all dressed up for an interview or something? Ha-ha, that's funny!

The life lessons I live by include; get a new job before you quit your old one and it never hurts to do a job interview from time to time.

My references were checked, so I was hopeful. The school year started and I didn't hear a word. Yeah, I was disappointed, but it was the farthest I had gotten with any job I had applied for.

Two weeks later, I checked my cell phone at lunchtime. I had a message to call the supervisor back. I went out to my car and called her. She told me that I did not get the job at the elementary school. They had chosen someone with more school nursing experience. I am thinking, "Wow, that was nice of her to let me know." The conversation wasn't over. She had another position and wondered if I would be interested in interviewing for it. It was four days a week working with 3-5 year olds in a quieter school. This program is called ECSE, Early Childhood Special Education. An "ah" came out of my mouth thinking about the little cuties! I needed to come for an interview as soon as possible. I interviewed for the position. I was even more relaxed this time; I knew the process. The next day I was offered the position. I called Steve quick and said, "What do you think?" "Take it!"

I put in my two-week notice and remembering my life lessons (never burn your bridges) went to a "casual call" status with homecare. Working for the hospital and homecare all these years had been good experience, they had been good to me and I made lifelong friendships.

I touched base with my supervisor on a start date, orientation and asked if it was okay if I went by "Nurse Kelly"? My last name is just too long. She said that was just fine. I had totally forgotten about the name of the book my aunt had given me so long ago. I was so excited! I am going to be a school nurse!

Chapter 6: What's in a name?

When my parents named me, Kelly was not a common name. I am told people made comments about it. At some point when I was little, I decided my name was Miss Flower, Miss Cauli-flower. Get it? My dad to this day still calls me Miss Flower. In elementary school, my last name Beecroft was subject to teasing. "Bee" or "Bee-crap", clever, huh? Stupid boys! In fourth grade one day we had to write poems. I had no idea, that my name would be used in several of my classmate's poems. Did you know Kelly rhymes with belly, smelly and jelly? It makes for a funny poem. I was not amused.

When we got married, my last name got considerably longer. I was happy to take Steve's last name, but I did not consider myself to me Mrs. Riemenschneider. I am Steve's wife and I am my own person, Kelly Riemenschneider. I didn't realize writing a check at any store was going to result in 20 questions or comments all the time. Wow, that's a long last name! "Gee, I had never noticed!" How many letters is that? How do you pronounce that? Is that German? Is "Riemen" the first name? How has Steve done it all these years? Nicole came along and then it was, "How long did it take her to learn how to spell that last name?" What ever happened to, "Nice day outside, huh?"

Everyone likes to take your name and shortening it to one syllable. I get called "Kel" all the time. I am fine with that. I have been called many things over the years, Kathy, Judy, and Kim. I still answer. I was one of several grandchildren. My grandma used to go down the list to get to my name, first calling me, Kathy, Mary, Diane, Cindy, Robin and sometimes even adding my mom's name Bonnie to the list. It never bothered me...I was her favorite! I am serious.

Soon after my mom found out I was pregnant, she made it clear she was not ok with being called "Grandma". When Nicole was old enough to start talking, I started trying to get Nicole to call her "Granny". I thought it would be hilarious or like I use to say when I was 3-1/2, "Funny, huh?"

Nicole being her own little person, started calling my mom Bummy. My mom's name is Bonnie, so she thought it was great! To this day, Nicole calls her Bummy and my mom signs Nicole's cards Love, Bummy and Grandpa.

Nicole always called me Momma when she was little. I loved it. I am mom now and that's good, too.

Chapter 7: Why is everyone smiling at me?

Now I was working a new job. The kids are adorable! I couldn't be happier. No stress. No Sunday nights dreading Monday morning and the new work week.

When I go out to run errands, people are looking at me and smiling. I am thinking, "What? Do I have something on my shirt?" It happens again and again. It took me some time to figure it out. It was me! I was happy and had a happy smiley face now! It is true what they say, "Smile and the whole world smiles with you."

I was encouraged to go into the classrooms and spend time with the children. I sat with them, played with them and just enjoyed their personalities.

The custodian came by the health office one day. He noticed I was smiling. He looked at me for a minute and finally said, "Do you ever stop smiling? What are you smiling about?" "I am smiling because I love my job. I am no longer stressed out. Life is good!" He walked away, probably thinking I was insane. As he walked away, I was thinking, "He probably thinks I am smiling because I take care of the kids when they are hurt or sick, but he is the one who has to clean up the blood and puke!"

School nursing has changed drastically over the years. Students that could not attend school are able to be an active part of the school population now. Diabetes, asthma, seizures and other health concerns can be managed at school. I can do suctioning, urinary catheterization, nebulizer treatments and give medications. Another reason to smile for me, I can do hands on care again.

I love to be creative and decorate. I was told that this was my health office; decorate it how you want. I brought chairs home to paint and put designs on. I went out and bought little cardboard monkey cutouts. Their tails hook together and they hook onto bananas. Fun, huh?

I bought a Mrs. Potato Head for on the counter. Another reason to smile. I like a good joke. It started happening on my Wednesdays when I was at ECSE. Mrs. Potato Head would show up in the refrigerator. That happened several times and no one would claim responsibility. Then, Mrs. Potato Head had Band-Aids all over and her arms were rearranged. No one would fess up. As a matter of fact, I was getting accused of the potato head abuse. On St Patrick's Day, she had on a green hat and someone took the time to take real baby potatoes, put eyes and green hats on them, too! Notes when back and forth. We figured it had to be the evening custodian. I confronted him, tripped him up and he confessed. He drives a school bus now!

Chapter 8: ECSE

It is a quieter school, but a good place to start for me. I had a student who I checked her hearing aids every day. When these little ones have been to the clinic or hospital for repeated care, they assume the school nurse is going to poke them and be no different than any other health office. Going down to the classroom to get to know them goes a long way. She didn't speak, but was learning sign language. I was learning sign language, too.

I did health screenings that include vision, hearing, height and weight checks. The cooperation level varies greatly. Some could not recognize shapes, yet others breezed right through it. Some students were more interested in the "special glasses", while others peeked or just plain got up and walked closer so they could see the shapes better. The hearing screen consists of putting a little earpiece in one ear at a time and getting a good seal with the right size rubber tip. It beeps and does all the work. It does have a trick to it and takes practice. Again, it was either a breeze or it was going to take several tries on several different days to test their hearing. Checking their weight could be like chasing a plastic bag in a gust of wind. When checking their height; are they standing straight or on their tip toes? Is their head straight or looking up; are their heels up against the wall? It could be like playing a game of Twister.

When I would come down to the classroom, most times the kiddos would just take my hand and go back to the health office with me for their screening. In one classroom, I had come down recently several times to get students. One little boy had already been screened, but each day I came back he would come up and ask me, "Do you need me to come with you?" When I told him no, I had already done his screening, he was clearly disappointed. From there on out I periodically would ask him if he could come with me or I would wait until he asked me and would tell him "yes". The smile on his face when he would walk down the hall with me was priceless. I usually gave him a sticker or checked his weight.

I have always had a soft spot for children with Downs Syndrome. I didn't realize how many health issues these kids can have and they generally can't feel pain like the rest of us. We had a student that loved to play hard and jump hard. The first time I saw him he had jumped off a slide sideways in the gym. Not even a tear. He was more upset that he had to be in my office. To get him to settle down, I let him go back to the classroom. To give you an idea how small these kids are, I used a tongue blade to splint his limp little arm. He had a compound fracture with a dislocated elbow. He would have many more minor accidents throughout the year. After a while, he called me by name, came to the health office willingly and I could put on an icepack.

I had several colds, fevers, tummy aches followed by puking. I had a couple of good lacerations that required a trip to the clinic. Nosebleeds are not uncommon either. Kids do not like having their nose pinched and certainly not an ice pack put on their nose if it won't stop.

At Early Childhood Special Education, when kids turn three they can start the program at any time during the year. We had a new little guy so excited to start school. These kids ride the bus and it is a BIG deal. I have even seen them cry when mom comes to pick them up and they can't ride the bus home that day. He did so well for his first day, he was escorted out to the bus to go home at the end of the day. The next thing I know, the teacher is bringing him into the office with a bloody nose. It was a pretty good bleeder. We needed to call mom to come pick him up. I got the bleeding to stop and he was leaning into my arm pretty hard. He was sound asleep! What an exhausting day.

Kids are so observant. Even at 3-5 years old they can sing the words to what is playing on the radio, they notice when I wear a new shirt and notice my dog on the computer screen wallpaper. They all want to see him and call him by name "Odd-iver" for Oliver. They do "high fives" and fist pumps. When I lost my voice one day, one little boy asked me what was wrong with my "froat".

They are all taught here to be polite, say hi, please and thank you. Some of these kids have been through more in their little lives then we could imagine. They want to touch you, have you sit down on their level and love to give you big hugs. I had one boy I hadn't seen in a little while. I said, "Hi, how are you?" He threw himself into me, hugging me and wrapping his legs around me so they were up off the floor.

I helped out for Family Literacy night. It is a chance for parents to spend time with their kids, learn the joy of reading and eat pizza together. I saw one of the boys from class. He is so darn cute. He has dark hair and glasses. He is shy and giggly. When he asks me a question he is always so serious. Tonight he came running up to me and says, "What are you doing here?" I bent down and said, " I came to help out tonight. The better question is what are you doing here?" He batted his long eyelashes at me, giggled and ran off. Melt my heart!

There is also a morning and afternoon preschool class in the building. I made the acquaintance of a Hispanic little lady killer with long curly hair in the morning class. He was always polite and has quite the little smile. He was sick one day, so I needed to have mom come pick him up. He talked non-stop to me in English while he was waiting in the health office. When mom came, he talked to her in only Spanish. This is why you start early with these kiddos if they are having learning issues, autism, behavior disorders or special needs. They pick things up a lot faster at this age. It blows my mind. From the beginning to the end of the school year you can see the progress that these students have made. It is amazing!

I had a little girl come in because her pierced ear looked infected. She was insistent that I could not take the earring out. I was able to finally get her to let me loosen the back and clean it up a bit. I called her mom to touch base. She has had her ears pierced for quite some time and hadn't worn earring for several months. Now all of a sudden, she wanted to wear earrings. The only way mom could take the earrings out was to do it at night after she fell asleep. That weekend Steve and I were out shopping in a small local shop. The little girl and her mom were also in the shop. She spotted me. She was pointing at me and mom was feeling uncomfortable. I walked up and greeted her by name, shook mom's hand and introduced myself. This was a positive thing that most of us take for granted. Coming out of their shell is a good thing.

The school year flew by. I didn't know how budgeting works in a school district. I was shocked to find out my job was being eliminated and changes were being made for next year.

Chapter 9: Transitional

I had only worked with the district one year and had no retention rights. I cried because I wasn't going to be working with the little ones, but oh crap, I have no job! This was not in line with my life lessons.

The school nurse fairy was looking out for me. A new position had opened up. It was working four days a week with 18-21 year olds in a transitional school and one day per week I could still work at ECSE. I went over and shadowed the nurse that was finishing up the current school year. I had to submit an application for the job. I had not so much as an interview as a "Meet and Greet" with the principal. I had large shoes to fill. I had worked in the oldest building in the school district with the youngest students. This school was the newest school with the oldest students in the district. Seems like a big difference, but not as much as you would think.

These students are in a transitional program. They go through high school graduation, but do not take their diploma. There are several reasons these students come to this program. Some have special needs; some have autism, behavior disorders, learning disabilities or just need some extra help to be independent self-sufficient adults. The school is based around a more business like atmosphere. The classes have reading, writing and math, but as it applies to being on your own in life. They learn to go grocery shopping, do laundry, cooking, and math as it relates to measuring ingredients. They learn how to fill out an application, do a job interview and how to dress for success, as they say. They study for getting their permit to drive, learn to comparison shop and look for housing. They graduate and get their diploma in one of two ways. If they meet their goals they can do an exit presentation and graduate any time during the year. They "age out" of the program when they turn 21. The philosophy of this learning program falls in line with my life lessons to be independent. I am totally on board.

Just as the little ones have gone through some horrible things, some of these students have heart-breaking stories. They are looking for acceptance and in some cases mothering. Several of these students have moved around or are in group homes. Sometimes it's more about the attention than the reason for the visit to the health office.

The new school year starts. Everyone is new to me once again and I need to learn names all over. The staff is very welcoming. Many of the students come up and introduce themselves. It is busier than ECSE. It is not nearly as busy as the other schools in the district, but as I soon found out, my job description would go beyond any boundaries you could imagine for a school nurse.

I had a student that was to get his medication shortly after arriving to school each day. It was easy for one day! He was not a morning person; he was not chatty or happy. He told me to "F" off the second or third day I was there. He was a challenge to be sure. My thinking out side the box began. By the end of the year, I could joke with him and we had an understanding. He called me nurse and I called him "just like the son I never had!"

I had a new office and again could set it up any way I wanted. I went for a more relaxing atmosphere. I brought a small water fountain and seashells, my radio, and put health teaching info on the walls. The students like the water fountain and the staff has finally stopped asking me, "Doesn't the sound of the water make you wanna pee?"

I made quick friends with another student who is tall and lean. He treats me like a mom. Some days, he can pester me to a fault, but I can take care of myself.

Just like when I worked at the hospital, you get "regulars" and get to know what to expect. We had a student that could make something out of nothing. I had a fish magnet in the bathroom and on the scale. She got so she said hi to them pretty much every day. She liked to exaggerate words. Fish became "feesh". She would come in and say hi to both "feesh", sometimes several times in a day. I brought in a pitcher and put ice water in it everyday.

I wanted students taking medications or just wanting a drink to have nice cold water. It became another reason to come see me. She told me and other staff that I made the best ice water, like there was some special trick to it. On the days I went to the other school, she took it on as her job to fill the water pitcher.

The students and staff just naturally started calling me Nurse Kelly. I like it! It feels like a badge of appreciation.

We had another student that always had the most unbelievable things happen to her. Her grandma died like ten times! Car accidents, someone punched her, she had a boyfriend, she didn't, she was engaged, and he died. One morning she came to school with fake vampire teeth in her mouth. She said she had been to a Halloween party the night before. The teeth were stuck in her mouth. There is no manual for this one. Google is my friend; I looked it up and found out how to get them out of her mouth. She still had to go to the dentist to get the remaining glue off her teeth. When she was actually in a car accident, it was like "the boy who cried wolf". No one believed her at first.

Students with multiple needs are generally fun loving and say and do the silliest things. There were two "peas in a pod" in the multiple needs class. They sang together, got crazy together and made you smile. One was into watching wrestling. He told everyone they were "a jabroni". The standard response was, "No you're a jabroni!" This could go back and forth several times. I asked other staff if that was a word and what it meant. No one seemed to know. Hello Google! A jabroni is a wrestler who loses in order to make another wrestler look good. Everyone has knowledge about the things they are interested in. He loved to sing and sounded good. He would say hi and serenade me with songs. His bro, his sidekick, his partner was equally entertaining. He liked to sing as well and the two of them could dance your socks off! He always greeted me, "Kelly, Kelly, Kelly! You are so awesome!" Don't be too impressed he told a lot of people that! He was always asking me to wash his hair and to shave, so he could look good for the LADIES! His hair was so short, but just like the newborns, washing his hair took thirty seconds, no blow dry needed. He wanted to shave regularly even though there wasn't even peach fuzz. I put shaving gel in his hand after he washed his face. He rubbed it all over his face; this included his nose and eyebrows! I gave him a disposable razor with the guard still on. Good thing, or he wouldn't have looked too good without eyebrows. Rinse, towel dry and then the standard line, "I look GOOD!"

The health office does border on a clinic. When students don't have insurance or a regular clinic, it is a problem. I have set up appointments with clinics for students, made eye appointments at a vision center that will do the exam and glasses for free if the student qualifies and set up dentist appointments. I soaked an infected toe every day and have done pre-natal teaching. I have found that YouTube has some great teaching videos.

Anger and frustration for the students is not uncommon. I have seen several students who have punched their fist into a wall, sometimes repeatedly. Their knuckles are red, bruised and quite swollen. Always keep lots of ice packs on hand.

Multiple needs students still bite at this age out of frustration, as I soon found out. Luckily, I haven't been bit yet. Staff gets bit from time to time and students bite other students. I had one the other day. She got too close and "chomp!" She had a perfect set of teeth mark bruises in her arm. It didn't break the skin, which was a good thing. It still hurts and is a surprise nonetheless.

The school is like a family; everyone worries about the other. When a student was having a bad day and sitting on the floor against a wall; I saw another student get right down on the floor with him. He only needed to say a couple joking words and the student snapped out of it. I saw a student sitting by herself at lunch; another student walked up and said, "Hi Doll-face! Can I sit by you?" You can't help but smile.

One thing I found out for sure, these students don't do well with change. A substitute for a staff member can throw the whole day off. I was still working at the other school on Wednesdays with the 3-5 year olds. It threw the students off. They got use to it, but it took time. I would do the "Wednesday shuffle" this year and part way into the next year before I was permanently stationed at the transitional school. Nurses are superstitious and believe the full moon affects births, illness and behaviors. At the hospital, births went up. At the school, students have more behaviors and stronger emotions. You can tell the full moon by the students, every time!

I love having a principal that lets the staff think outside of the box. Nicole asked me if I wanted some clothes for students when she was going through her clothes. It sparked an idea. I collected gently used clothes and other items. I put together a Girl's Boutique before Christmas, so the girls could get needed clothes and accessories. I thought it would be a great teachable moment. I priced all the items and gave the girls fake money to spend. The girls had a great time and wanted to know when we could do it again. I was worried I wouldn't be able get enough donations to do it again. Be careful what you wish for! I ended up having so many items the next year that I sent items on to another school in the district and they had a small boutique, too.

Fair is only fair: I needed to do something for the guys. I call it Man Cave Casino. I made a nerf obstacle course. They had to hit a stack of pop cans, plastic cups and wall targets. I talked the principal into letting us trace her onto paper. The multiple needs class made her hair, and an outfit. The guys loved hitting the "flat principal". Even the principal went through the course. Dang, she is good. She hit "flat principal" no sweat! They played black jack and other games to win tickets. Who likes doing math? It was another way to do math in a fun way. All the prizes were won by redeeming the tickets. Shirts, baseball hats, snacks and other guy items. They get pretty loud. Year two I made some changes, like making the nerf obstacle course bigger. It was the Zombie obstacle course and it went down the length of a hallway.

I figured as the school nurse I should do a health fair. I want to teach them about good hand washing, get their height and weight, check their blood pressure, teach them good oral hygiene and show them food serving sizes. Did you know seven French fries are considered a serving? Who eats only seven fries? I wanted to see if I could get some items donated. I found out it never hurts to ask for donations and most times I am successful. I got toothbrushes, toothpaste, eyeglass cleaner and an assortment of other items. It isn't the funniest thing the students have ever done, but I caught a couple high blood pressures. These students had follow ups at their clinics which included EKG's, lab work and scans. I got the ok to buy goggles that simulate what it feels like to be drunk. It is a great tool. It goes along with my other station that the students get measured amounts of Hawaiian Punch to see how much they can drink before being considered legally drunk. You actually have to stay close to the student with the goggles on; they can't even walk a straight line!

These students are invited every year to participate in prom at another school in a totally different school district. This beautiful old school is rich in history and has the most amazing high school students. They plan the whole event and it is beautiful. The students are stationed throughout the school to assist their invited guests throughout the evening. They direct traffic, help out in the bathroom and are "planted" on the dance floor. Groups of guys and gals walk around on the crowded dance floor looking for students dancing stag. They walk up and enthusiastically ask if they want to dance with them. It is so sweet. Our students, all dressed up, look fabulous. No asking them twice if I can take their picture. I am like a proud mom! Before the prom, I asked Steve if he would go with me. I really wanted to go see the students. He said, "Are you asking me to prom?" "Yes." "I'll have to think about it!" When students asked if I was going, I told them how Steve had teased me. They thought it was pretty funny.

One of the girls that went to prom would have never done this if not for the great work of the staff at school. She was so shy, they tell me she barely talked. The girl I know, talks all the time. She was at prom and looked beautiful. She was just standing on the sideline. I went over and talked to her. She asked me if I wanted to "boogie-woogie" with her. Twice we went out and danced. She was having fun. A group of the high school students came up and asked her if she wanted to dance with them. She agreed and told me; I could go rest, she would be fine! She just asked me the other day if I was going to prom this year. "Do you remember last year when we really cut up the dance floor?"

Students with autism can be very difficult to carry on a conversation with. It is awkward for them. Many conversations are carried out with yourself. On this particular day, I was trying to engage a student in conversation. He answered my questions, but never offered any more than necessary. We hit a silence in the conversation. He looked at me and said, "We are done talking now, you can leave."

Communication can take on many forms with students here. I have learned a little sign language, hand signals, turning everything into yes or no questions and reading other signals. One student likes to just point his finger at me and then toward the health office; meaning I need to see you in your office. If he points to the medication cupboard, he wants two of his Advil. Some times he tilts his head in the direction of my office. The other day, he lifted is eyebrows in that direction.

My daughter still has me give her shots every two weeks for her disorder. Sometimes, it works out better for her to come to school. The students all treat her like part of the family. One student who liked to come see me every day just to "shoot the breeze" saw Nicole come in one day. He walked up and I introduced him. Nicole shook his hand. He looks at me and without skipping a beat says, " We did a good job with this girl!" Then he looks at her and tells her she is grounded! He graduated at the end of the year, but still stops by to visit and asks, " How is our daughter, Nicole?"

Steve does a great job with woodworking projects. Steve always rolls his eyes when I utter the words, "I was thinking…" This time it was to make a wood bench for outside my office so the staff and students could sit there at break time or when my door is closed and they are waiting to see me. I got the principal's approval. Every time I see people sit on it, I smile.

I had this great idea to make a Zen Garden for the students. Steve made the box to put the sand in and the little rake. I would bring sand back from Florida when we were on vacation. I got the sand and found shells from the beach to put in the garden. I put the sand in a zip lock bag and put it in the travel bag for the flight home. Steve went through security first. He was talking to the TSA after he got through. I figured it was small talk and didn't think much of it. I went through the scanner. I am standing next to Steve. The TSA holds up the bag of sand and asks me if it is mine. I said yes. She then asks me if I know that it is illegal to bring sand back. I am pretty sure my mouth dropped open. I looked at Steve and said, "Well, I guess I will be staying in Florida!" The TSA looks at Steve and then at me. "He said you would be a good sport and ok with a joke." Excuse me while I go change the jeans I just wet! The Zen Garden is in the Behavior Specialist's office. Some students thought it was dumb at first. Soon they find out it is hard to put the rake down.

Chapter 10: Patient teaching

Educating my patients is a big part of my job. At the hospital I did diabetic teaching, post heart attack teaching, baby care instructions and gave hospital discharge instructions.

At school, the teaching is much broader. I teach with posters, displays and PowerPoint presentations. I do one on one teaching, classroom and staff teaching. I have done prenatal teaching, nutrition, hygiene and oral care. All the staff works to show them how to do laundry, ironing, work the dishwasher, run the microwave and using the oven. I have even helped students study for health related tests. I have been asked how to ask someone out. I've been asked how to break up with someone. I have discussed what to look for when buying a puppy. What it feels like to be numb from Novocain and what an elephant eats.

I have handouts for head injuries and head lice. You'd be surprised how many times I have had to check for head lice because, "My head itches!" One of the classes at ECSE had a possible lice issue. To make everyone feel better, I checked every student in that class. I didn't want to cause alarm, so I did it right in the classroom. I told the kids their teacher had spilled glitter and I needed to check their hair for "glitter." They couldn't wait for me to check their hair. "Do I have any glitter in my hair?"

Thankfully, no!

Chapter 11: Nurse MacGyver

Being a smaller school, you need to work as a team and work beyond your job description. I have extra clothes and undergarments as needed. I have pants and shirts for volunteer/work sites. I do laundry and help keep the student kitchen clean. I help with breakfast and lunch. You work with what you have on hand. I mend clothes, hats and purses. I have been asked if I have an earring to match the one they lost, do you have a belt, shoes, deodorant, a comb, hair binder, lint brush, static guard, a water bottle, pop, change for a $5, change for a $10, ...I wash hair, cut fingernails, toenails, and hair.

While I am clearly not a clinic or drugstore, I do my best. Steve has been known to call me Nurse MacGyver. When a student asked me if I had any Proactiv for his face, I made my own. I have used duct tape to hold shoes together, a paper clip for repairing an eyeglass stem, ribbon for straps on a prom dress, old jeans to make patches, a spot Band-Aid for a missing nosepiece. It becomes a challenge, what can I use that will work?

I love the website Pinterest. I have gotten ideas from there. A student that wears a bandage to protect an area on her back, I made a sports bra out of underwear and padded the area that needed the bandage and tape on her skin all the time.

I think we have all ripped out a pair of pants at one time or another. It can be rather embarrassing. We'll call this student "Ripper". He has ripped out five different pairs of jeans. The first time, it was the end of the day. He came in, "You ARE NOT going to guess what just happened? I ripped my jeans!" I didn't even have a chance to answer. He changed out of them and I actually took the stapler and stapled the hole shut so he could get home. "Does it show? Can you see it?" You really couldn't. The second time, "You ARE NOT going to believe what happened! I ripped my jeans!" By the third time to the fifth time, we were both getting use to it! "Guess what? It happened again!" We both smile and just laugh! The last time, I made my own jean batch and hand sewed it over the rip. "Can you see where it ripped?" "No." Me neither!" "Thanks, Kelly!"

Tennis shoes being in need of repair are a regular visit to my office. I treat the soul some days and Nurse MacGyver fixes the sole on others. Super glue is a valuable tool.

I also feel the need to think outside the box when treating students. I use a holistic approach. I use relaxation breathing; gentle stretching, simple massage, hot tea with honey and I recently added aromatherapy. Whether it actually works or not isn't important. What is important is that it makes them feel better.

I also have another very scientific way of treating "aches and pains" that students complain of. They come to see me; I ask them what's going on? They say, "It hurts when I do this." My answer is always the same, "Then don't do that any more. Problem solved!"

Being a mom, I have hats, scarves, mittens and jackets on hand. Some students don't have these items and some just don't think they need to wear them. I have had them come in soaking wet from rain or snow. I dry their clothes and give them something to wear in the mean time. Never under estimate the age that students stop falling into the mud; I am just sayin'!

Chapter 12: I am a staff nurse, too

Staff members get sick and hurt at school as well. Some staff have chronic conditions that I keep an eye on. I have had lacerations and possible concussions; falls, cracked ribs, bruises, fractures, sprains, rashes, headaches and blood pressure checks. A teacher came to school one morning and was waiting for me when I got to school. Her cat got scared and in the excitement clawed her up pretty good. Those types of bites and scratches are very susceptible to infection. After I cleaned up and covered her wounds, I made sure she set up an appointment to be seen sooner than later and get on antibiotics. Her ear had been scratched as well. She ended up needing to have a plastic surgeon stich that ear.

One staff member has a heart condition and diabetes. When she gets stressed she wants to eat sweets. She is older than me, but that doesn't mean I am not going to get after her! We are a family; I worry just the same. She will tell me, "I am stressed, don't look Kel!" "Put that down!" Sometimes she barters with me, "Split it with me?" Sometimes it works.

I have taken stiches out for staff members. I have taken my own stiches out. You keep those covered. Students worry. I had a small lesion removed off my wrist. Students asked me about it or they wanted to touch it.

One student came right out and asked me if it was cancer. "That wouldn't be good if you had cancer." I assured her it was not cancer.

Chapter 13: Funny, huh?

I have always had a sense of humor. It helps me get through uncomfortable situations and keeps things light.

My brother and I had the usual sibling rivalry when growing up. We called each other names, teased and pestered each other. The teasing still continues, and the occasional pinching with salad tongs.

My mom has had her occasional moments, probably because we drove her to it. One night I was washing dishes and turned around to see her with cold cooked spaghetti noodles hanging from her nose! I didn't know whether to laugh or be afraid.

Nicole picked up on that as well. After we went to see the movie "Night at the Roxbury". We about drove Steve crazy! Every time we were in the car after seeing that movie, we were bobbing our head to one side in unison. If I were being too serious in the car, Nicole would be in the passenger seat making faces and dancing to some snappy tune on the radio. I would eventually catch her out of the corner of my eye, turn my head and she's act like she wasn't doing anything.

In high school Nicole regularly used the phrase, "Back in the day" when she was talking about something that happened in the past. Steve and I use to laugh; she doesn't have enough years on earth to be coining that phrase. When I learned you could "buy" an ad in the yearbook, I bought a small space in her senior yearbook. I found the cutest picture I could find of her when she was little and coined her phrase below it. Did I tell her and spoil the surprise? Nope. "MOM, what did you do?"

I am not really sure how it started, probably over a conversation about how tacky my mom and I find plastic yard flamingoes. It started with two of them, then flamingo twinkle lights, add a plastic penguin and we are on a full out flamingo war! I put them in their bathtub and filled it with balloons; they came back on my back deck. They were back in my parent's bed with the twinkle lights, only to return when I am getting ready to have company. We have a mutual friend who got involved and fifty flamingoes were on the front lawn for my mom on Mother's Day. The funny part of that one was that my dad wanted to cut the grass that day. He picked them all up, cut the grass and then put them back only for the service company to pick them back up in the middle of the night! I could get all technical and say that I am left-handed and that causes this creative flow. It isn't that complicated, I am just competitive and want the last laugh. The flamingo wars ended in a truce shortly after I ramped things up a notch. I was given a pink toilet and hence the scene on the front lawn was created. Pink toilet, penguin in toilet; penguin holding Christmas garland reins connected to the pink flamingoes out ahead of the toilet like Santa and his sleigh. People were pulling over, looking at it and taking pictures. They live on a busy road. My momma was not happy with me, but you must admit it is funny!

We are currently on a gnome truce. She's over there right now, like a pack rat, all the goods; just waiting for the perfect time to bring them home to the mother ship! I am watching you!

We have had the same veterinarian for a number of years. He is down to earth, sensible and has a good sense of humor as well. When I took Oliver in for one of his shots in the series of puppy shots, we talked about his oral care. He asked me if I brush his teeth. I told him I do, every day. He thought he was going to pull a fast one on me, "Do you use your toothbrush to brush his teeth?" I was on my game that day and retorted, "No, I use Steve's toothbrush!"

Things can get pretty serious at school. I have had days when it was hard to hold back the tears. One student lost his mom when he was in elementary school. I am sure he wonders what life would have been like if she was still here. Once in a while he comes to school with a chain around his neck. On that chain is a little picture frame with a picture of his mother in it. She was beautiful. Every time he sits in my office and is wearing that, I acknowledge his mother. I just hold the frame in my fingers, and tell him how beautiful his mother was. We're good and ten minutes later he is usually poking me in the arm repeatedly, saying, "Hey, hey, hey, hey…" or doing karate kicks toward me. Standard operating procedure is for me to grab his foot and hold it up in the air. He loves to joke around, but he also feels the need to touch me in some way. He is tall, so it is usually a squeeze to my arms from behind.

Students love to tell jokes and after the punch line say, "Do you get it?" I have been in a long running game of "tag" with a student. I tried the "You're it, I quit" line, but it didn't work! He will tap me repeatedly so he makes himself it or am I it? Students like to scare you or poke you on the opposite shoulder that they are standing by. I don't scare very easily, but I have fallen for the shoulder tap. All this poking, it is a wonder I don't have bruises on my arms!

The staff is very lighthearted as well. I work with a paraprofessional (Para) during breakfast and lunch each day. She likes to sing. She sings little ditties that I usually have never heard; most have a funny little twist. We call each other names all the time. Yesterday, she called me "Nursie-poo". I countered with "Para-poo". She replied, " That sounds cute!" "Yeah, it sounds like one of those fancy dog breed mixes, a Para-poo!"

At the end of each school year the students get to throw whip cream pies in the faces of staff members. It is part of a fundraiser for the end of the year school party. It is done outside and it is a sticky mess! The students love it. I will admit, I don't volunteer for this event. The students are brutal and have a bit too much fun! Could it be that I can't have the last laugh? They have also done carwashes in the past. The water hose does end up other places than on the cars they are washing.

Laughing and keeping it light is another one of my life's lessons.

Chapter 14: Grandma and me

We lived an hour away from my grandparents. We went to their house for regular visits, holidays and I would stay two weeks at a time over the summer when I was young.

My creative hand came from my grandma. She was amazing! She would sew Barbie doll clothes for me with no pattern!

We always went to the little corner store and I got to pick out whatever candy I wanted. My sweet tooth started young. Grandma always took me "visiting." I learned how to chat and sip hot tea. I also learned what, "Don't tell anyone!" meant. One time we were driving home on a dirt road in the middle of nowhere. She decided to turn around in the middle of the road. In the process, we went into the ditch. We both looked at each other with big eyes of surprise. She pulled forward only to go into the opposite ditch. Again, we looked at each other and started laughing. When she got the car back on the road, she swore me to secrecy! This is the first time I ever told anyone, that's been a long time ago!

Grandma had a china head doll. It was always wrapped in a baby blanket upstairs in the fourth dresser drawer. I took care of babies carefully even back then. I was always allowed to bring the doll downstairs all by myself. The doll had been my grandma's since she was young. She had been saved through a fire and a tornado over the years.

The Christmas before my grandma passed away, she gave only one present that year. She had had a stroke and speaking was difficult. The present was for me. It was the blonde haired china head doll. It was a gift of love attached with many memories. To this day, I have the doll in a glass display case that sits on my dresser. She has a handkerchief on her lap that was my grandma's with her name written on the corner "Kitty", which was short for Kathryn.

I was afraid of thunderstorms when I was young. Grandma always had a way of calming my fears. She told me they were just "people bowling in the clouds." I haven't been afraid since.

Grandma made a lot of homemade goodies and I like to do that, too. We liked to tease each other and laugh. Most of all, I liked to play and tease my grandpa. He was such a good sport. I guess the medical profession was in the back of my head even way back then. He most often was my patient when I was the dentist or the doctor. Funny, huh?

My grandparents nurtured me and gave me the life lesson that they liked me just the way I was. I thought the world of them. In their later years, they needed to go to a nursing home. We wrote back and forth between visits. She would always tell me they didn't belong there with "all these old people!" When my grandma died, two weeks later my grandpa was found dead, unable to live without her.

Many years have passed and I still think about them. After some time, some of my grandma's things were found and divided up. One of the things I was given was a pink pearl necklace with a beautiful clasp. I wore it to Steve's company Christmas party. I got up to use the restroom during the evening. When I looked in the restroom mirror, I noticed pink flecks all over on my neck. Turns out they weren't real pearls! Good one Grandma! I sprayed them with several coats of varnish two years ago, so I could wear them at Nicole's wedding. I also put a handkerchief of grandma's in Nicole's bridal bouquet.

One other piece of jewelry was given to me later. It was like a piece of treasure from a sunken treasure chest. Over all the years my grandma always wore just a wedding band. Turns out she had an engagement ring. The diamond had been removed and placed into another ring by my aunt. My mom took that ring, having something of her sister's and her mother's diamond all in one. I had a new diamond set into the old ring. I wear it all the time. It brings me untold comfort. Students at ECSE and the Transitional school find comfort in that ring as well. I have had several students hold my hand and gently turn the ring back and forth on my finger. Love you grandma!

The pranks had to come from somewhere. After my aunt passed away, I was told about the "ugly necklace" that went back and forth as a gift for years between my mom and her. End of story, not yet! My uncle found the necklace and sent it to me the next year to wrap up and give to my mom for Christmas. Surprise!

Chapter 15: Shopping tips

I was always game to help and be with my dad. Up on the roof, out in the pasture, I was a true tomboy. As I got older, I would go with my dad to help him go Christmas shopping for my mom. The trip was an outing that always started with stopping for coffee and a donut. He was teaching me about taking work breaks; I just never paid attention to that lesson. We would go from store to store. To his credit, he usually had a gift in mind.

My feet are the same size as my mom, so one year I was trying on boots, boots and more boots. I would come stumbling out of the dressing room with boots that fit my feet but not my chicken legs. The sales clerk would remark how nice they looked on me. Are you kidding me?

One year my dad decided to get my mom a new wedding band. How convenient, my ring size is the same. We went from jewelry store to jewelry store until my dad couldn't take it any more. Each time I would try a ring on, they would look at my dad, then at me and raise their eyebrows. By the third or fourth store, he told me to wait outside the store for him. Really, you can't tell he's my dad?

I learned three important life lessons to add to my list from shopping with my dad. If your dad tells you he can "smell out a coffee shop" he is not kidding. A sales clerk will tell you anything to sell you a pair of boots and

lastly, if he is about to make a bad gift decision, DON'T LET HIM DO IT!
These days, he has gotten smart. I am his personal shopper. I buy the gift
and wrap it.

I like to go shopping, but apparently I have an approachable look. I
once had a woman walking in my direction at the mall say "Hi." She was
kind of looking at me. I didn't know her. I looked around; there was no one
else but me. She actually yelled at me that she had said hi to me. She was
scary! I said hi and kept on going. Yikes!

Then there was the first time I witnessed mental illness or maybe it
was a grocery store breakdown. The woman had a grocery cart and she was
up by the deli counter. Something set her off and she started yelling and
flipped the grocery cart upside down. I'm ready to check out now!

I went to a pizza place. I was just about to walk in to order a pizza to
go. One of the employees came out and had fire in her eyes. She started
throwing the metal chairs around outside. I always have said that at least if I
went to hell, I'd be warm, you didn't tell me it would be dangerous and I
would have to worry about what they may have done to my pizza.

I sometimes feel like I have "nurse" tattooed on my forehead. I get
approached to open plastic bags, reach this off the shelf; do you know where

this is or how that works? When people learn I am a nurse they automatically want advice.

I get embarrassed for other people. I once saw a lady in a department store walk right into a stationary pole and say excuse me. I felt so bad for her I couldn't even look at her. I did peek and she was ok.

I had a neighbor call me up once and ask if I would go over and give his mom an enema. I missed the lesson on how to tactfully say no. What a novel idea, homecare. I wish I had thought of that.

Chapter 16: Sometimes there are no words

I became a nurse for the same reason many do, to care for other people. It comes naturally; it's not something I have to think about.

After Steve's grandpa's funeral there was a luncheon in the church basement. Being a nurse, I was the obvious choice to take his grandma to the restroom. We got into the handicap stall and I helped her out of her wheelchair and onto the toilet. When I helped transfer her back to the wheelchair, I had her hold on to the grab bar on the wall. The grab bar broke away from the wall during the transfer. His grandma and I looked at each other and started laughing. It lightened a sad day. I was sworn to secrecy. Where have I heard that before? This is the first time I have told anyone.

We are at the funeral. He is elderly, his head is bent in sorrow and he stands alone for the service in front of a closed casket. No one knows what to do or say. I can't stand it. I walk up and put my hand on the small of his back and hand him a tissue. I don't say a word sometimes you don't need to.

I have found an interesting thing that occurs when I go to a funeral. The power of touch is very strong. I walk up, extend my hand and offer condolences. My hand remains clutched by the bearer as they speak. Soon their other hand has reached over and is gently rubbing my arm or hand. This has happened several times.

We were at a funeral for a son who had died tragically. He loved rock music. It was cold so I had on my Hard Rock leather jacket. I spoke to his brother and he was drawn to rub the arm sleeve of my jacket between his fingers while we talked. His mom was exhausted. She had taken her shoes off for comfort. As we spoke, she reached out and grabbed my jacket sleeve, rubbing it between her fingers. I see this as a comfort. I let them take the lead. When they are ready they will let go.

Over the years of taking care of patients and students the life lessons are the same. You don't always have to show you care with words. Sitting down next to someone, rubbing their shoulder or holding their hand can be enough. Students will turn the rings on my fingers or play with my necklace as we sit together.

Chapter 17: The Gatekeeper

At our school we are all gatekeepers. We all have our role, plus a little more. As the school nurse I am the gatekeeper of the District's policies and the Health Department's regulations. Some days it does not make me very popular with parents. I have parents yell, swear and hang up on me. Everyone wants to be liked, that doesn't always happen.

A student that was sick told me one day that his mom didn't like me. I live by the life lesson of the Golden Rule: Treat others, as you want to be treated. When I answered the student, I added another life lesson to my list. I told him, "I am a big girl. If she doesn't like me, that's ok. I care about you, and your health. I want you to always feel you can come to me when you aren't feeling well." I still think about the day I told him that. The bottom line is the students and if someone doesn't like me, that is the way it is.

The students like to use my bathroom. It is more convenient than going all the way down the hall. They are always polite and ask if they can use the bathroom. I was talking to one student in my office and another one came in. He breezed past us and said, "Thanks, Kels!" The other student was perplexed. I explained, "I know he is going to ask to use the bathroom and he knows I am going to say yes, so he is just cutting to the chase!"

When I help with breakfast and lunch I can tell how staff and students feel by how they look when they come in each morning. It is no surprise when they want to see me in my office.

At lunch, we have a couple of students that eat like it's the only meal they ever get. I know that is not true, they usually have an objective behind it. One student eats so fast, the Para from her classroom gives her a straw to drink her milk slower and cuts all her food in small pieces to try and slow her down. She loves pop and will come in to see me and tell me she needs her inhaler. I always check students out first, it's my job, but she fakes a lot! She loves pop. She will see my can of pop, point and say, "Pop please!" I will usually, ok, I will always give in and give her a small paper cup of pop. I always tell her to "Savor it" but it is usually all gone by the time I get out "Sav".

As I am standing behind the lunch counter, she is eating her lunch. She keeps putting more food in her mouth. She looks like a chipmunk with her cheeks as full as she can get. As a mom and nurse, I can't stand it. I walk over, put my hand on her shoulder, lean down and tell her she has plenty of time to eat lunch, slow down, I don't want you to choke. Her mouth is so full she just nods. I walk back behind the lunch counter. She is chewing,

chewing, turns her head away from me and adds just another teeny weeny bite, and another and another….

I am also the gatekeeper of student's belongings. The backpacks and purses are left with our secretary at the front desk. I get the drinks, change of clothes, house keys, money, cell phones and MP3 players. Usually the cell phones and MP3 players have no battery life left. That is awful! They can't live without them. As Nurse MacGyver, I have a cord for that! These belongings are very important. I get a lot of, "Can you keep this for me and DON'T LET ANYONE touch it!" I always answer, "Ok!" while I take my fingertip and touch the item! "Hey, Kelly! Not funny!"

The same as any young adult, many sleep until the last minute, jump out of bed and don't have time for breakfast before heading off to school. Some just plain don't have much food in the house. We try to keep snack and food items on hand for just that reason. They may present with a stomachache or a headache. The first question is, "Did you eat breakfast?" Some are more direct, and politely ask for something to eat. They act like it is a MacGyver thing. "She has everything!"

Chapter 18: Taking a compliment

Midwesterners are known for not being able to just accept a compliment. We will even argue, "No, no." Compliments come in all shapes and forms. I am always amazed when a perfect stranger; whether it be a cashier or someone standing next to me will give me a compliment. I was taught growing up to never talk to strangers. I have been told that they like my necklace, my shirt, my haircut, and those shoes look comfortable. It is a true compliment. They don't know me; they aren't obligated to say anything nice to me.

When I went out shopping for a dress for Nicole's wedding, I went by myself. I had an idea what I wanted: A dress that doesn't look like a mother of the bride dress from 1900, not too long, not too short, not too revealing, not too prudish, not too expensive and looks flattering. It wasn't as bad as it sounds. I went to one mall and had plenty of options. When I found a dress that I liked, I wanted to be sure it would be acceptable. A mother and college age daughter came in the dressing room area at the same time as me. I decided to talk to strangers and ask for a no obligation opinion. They were flattered! They were more than happy to give an opinion. Since it was a vintage wedding, the daughter suggested I go to a vintage store to find a sweater or wrap to wear over the dress when it gets chilly in the evening.

We have a couple of students that moved here from the south when they were young. You can always tell. They call me "Miss Kelly." I like it! It feels like a compliment of respect.

A few days ago, a student asked me how long I had worked at the school. I answered his question, end of conversation. He came back and asked me today how long I am going to work here. I told him I planned to work here a long time. "Good, 'cause I'm here for two more years!" It takes a while to figure out a student's style of approach. He also asked me if I had a nail clipper one day. I got it out of the drawer as I told him yes. He told me he didn't need it; he just wanted to know if I had one. The next day, he asked me to cut his nails. He tests the water first and then asks me what he wants to know. When someone trusts you that is a big compliment.

We are selling ice cream cones this afternoon in the cafeteria. He has to go to work at a volunteer site this afternoon. He comes in and gives me money and politely asks if I would buy two ice cream cones for him before they are all gone. It is a compliment in trust. I don't ever mind.

Chapter 19: A new year, some new students and a new set of things you can't make up!

It's my second year at the transitional school. I know what to expect, but there are always surprises! Our new students are all pretty close to each other. Two of the students act like siblings. They fight, punch, tease, hug and help each other out. They often come in my office and complain, "He's picking on me" or "Are you going to let him get away with that?"

Leg braces use to come in plain issue white, now they are called AFO's (Ankle Foot Orthotic) and come in all colors and designs. I have a student who takes his skull head patterned AFO's off in my office and leaves them with me depending on what activity he is going to be doing. I try my best not to step in and help him unless he asks. I have to literally sit on my hands some times. He will finally look up at me and say, "Go for it Kel!"

Then there is the new student that I am not sure who I like more, him or his mom! She has so much patience. Everything with this big brown eyed, long lash student goes into his mom's "Adventure file". He is very animated and talks non-stop. The day he came to school so tired that he was literally laying his head down on the table and falling asleep, was not usual. Turned out he accidently took his evening meds that morning. Mom just laughed.

I just about got myself stuck in a corner with him one day. He asked me if I had ever heard of the Avengers movie? I said, "Yes." Where I got in trouble was when he went on to ask me who was my favorite super hero from the movie. I wasn't sure which super heroes were in the movie, so I asked him, "Who is your favorite?" "Why, Captain America of course!" I am nodding my head, being all cool, "Yup, that's a good choice!"

There was the day I started helping him with nail care. When I asked him how he cut his toenails, he showed me. He put his foot right up to his mouth. All I could say was, "Geez, you are flexible! Let's not do it that way any more!" Oh, and the day he was brushing his teeth. He stopped and had his hand in his mouth. I thought the floss broke. I asked if he needed a new piece of floss. Nope, he was trying to put something back into his mouth. He wanted to know if I had any glue or something to put a piece of his tooth back in place. Mom wasn't even surprised! What a woman!

I never can be sure if the students are serious or pulling my leg, so I have to stay on my game. I had a student come in and seriously said, "My fingers are green. What's wrong?" I looked at them for a minute and put her hands under the water faucet. "I don't know, but nothing serious. See, it washed off!"

I checked a height for a student one day. He asked me how tall he was. When I replied 5'2", he looked at me and said, "Still 5'2", typical Asians!"

A student was sent to my office one day because he had been watching a video in class and he thought it was so funny he couldn't stop laughing. He was laughing so hard he was getting a headache. It took me 10 minutes to get him to stop laughing and be able to send him back to class. The subject of the video was about "taking short cuts" like home from school. This kid was cutting through the back alley and there were two bums in the alley. The one talked funny and his nickname was "Mushroom." This was enough to cause him uncontrolled laughter. No one else in the class seemed to find it funny.

At Halloween time, a scavenger hunt through the school was planned. I was asked if they could use my office. I agreed and a talking plastic skeleton was placed on the far cot with a blanket over him. The curtain was pulled. They needed to get the next clue from under the skeleton. When I told the students there was no heart beat and asked them to see what they thought, most of them were very skeptical. Some jumped, some hung onto my arm. The multiple needs class was fearless. They would rip the blanket off, then laugh and laugh!

The health office is not a clinic as I said before, but that doesn't mean that I haven't had some hairy moments. I had a student who had a seizure and another who took a nasty fall about the same time. The day I will never forget was the day one of our students missed the bottom step at another school and fell. They brought her back in the van. She didn't cry until she saw my face. Her ankle was swelling up so fast I knew it wasn't good. I calmed her down and needed to hold ice on it. Then a second student came in with a nosebleed. It was really bleeding! I held the ice on the ankle with one hand and the other was pinching his nose. He was comforting the other student. When a third student came in for their morning medication, I had no hands left. I verbally flagged down a staff member that was walking by the window of the office. I had her reach in my pocket and get the key to the medication cupboard and walked her through giving the student his medication.

I am the hand washing police. When "little missy" comes in to use the bathroom, I always need to ask her if she washed her hands when she is done. On this particular day, we went back and forth. "Did you wash your hands?" She replies yes, yes she is sure and by the third time she looks at me and says, "I AM SURE MOM!"

Hygiene is an issue for any student starting in about middle school. One week they are cleaning up and looking sharp, the next week, they roll out of bed late and show up to school with their hair sticking straight up. Some I need to work with, while others it suddenly "clicks in" and they start taking pride in their appearance. One student that it has "clicked" for goes to a technical college for a class and then is with us for classes the other part of his day. He is learning auto repair. You do get dirty and smell like oil. It is part of the job. He comes in to see me often to ask me if it is dirt or oil on his jeans, how do I get this cleaned off, is this noticeable? One day he asked me if he smelled. I told him he smelled like oil, but that would be expected and I like that smell. "So, you are saying I smell?"

When I talked to this student last year, all he could do is swear when he talked to me. This year, he is a new person. He even apologized for all the swearing last year. His greeting to me is, "Hi Doc!" I told you I answer to anything. He cracks me up. He came in one day because his ankle hurt. He explains that he has hurt this ankle before. It was a very logical conversation until; he asked me if he was going to lose his leg. I told him no and he looked disappointed. His hope was to get a wooden leg and then he could kick people with it!

I have had sick students in the bathroom. This time it was in the men's bathroom. Nauseated and throwing up, he had been in there for a while. When he was not able to come out, I crawled under the stall and unlocked the door. I got him to the point where we could go back to the health office. You would have thought coming in after him would have mortified him, but it didn't. I get regular hugs from him.

A student came in my office complaining of constipation. The next day, he still didn't feel right. He was in class and announced he was sick with constipation and headed to my office. After he left, another student in the class wanted to know if it was contagious.

Students come in and out of my office all the time to get a drink, a Band-Aid or sometimes just to talk. A student told me one day that he liked talking to me. "You talk to me like an adult." This as he hopped up on the counter and is swinging his legs.

I like to talk to the students when I am with them. I asked this student if she spoke Hmong at home? She only speaks English at school. She told me, "No, not very much." Then I asked her if her cat spoke Hmong. I thought she was crying at first. She was laughing so hard; tears were rolling down her face. The next day when I took care of her, she couldn't wait to tell me about her cat. He speaks Spanish!

We have had a lot of sore throats and coughing this winter. I don't even have to ask what they need. When I got the "Ricola" cough drops, I decided to change it up for fun. The students sing "Ri-co-la" to me when they come in.

Just like home, the bathroom sink and mirror can get to be a mess. A student came in to brush his teeth. When he was done he told me, "What a bunch of pigs! I am a gentleman and clean up after myself." He wiped up around the sink and left. The mirror and sink however, were still full of toothpaste.

A student came into the bathroom today to use the bathroom. While he was in there, I heard him say, "Uh, Ah-Oh!" I answered back, "Are you okay?" "Yeah, I am fine!" There was a pause. I asked, "What Ah-Oh?" "How do I explain this?" I asked him if he dropped his cell phone in the toilet. "No, nothing like that!" He finally told me that the toilet paper roll was almost empty. I told him there was another roll on the bottom of the wood shelf in there. "Oh, I see it!" There is another pause, "I don't know how to put the new roll on!" "That's ok, I can do it." "Ok!" I was so surprised. No student has ever put a new roll of toilet paper on, let alone is concerned about it!

Back when I was in high school, the movie Monty Python and the Holy Grail was popular. When my daughter was in high school, the movie Monty Python and the Holy Grail was popular. Guess what? It is popular with this generation, too. Imagine their surprise when I can recite lines from the movie. They don't realize how long this movie has been around. For a couple of students, lines from the movie are almost a daily greeting in the halls. The best day was when I put a sign up outside my office telling two certain students that they could not enter until they answered "the three questions." What is your name, what is your quest, what is your favorite color? I could hear them laughing before I even saw their faces.

I always tease that I run with scissors. I don't really ever do that. Accidents do happen with scissors. A student was cutting one day with a scissors and she cut her finger. It wasn't a horrible cut, but it didn't want to stop bleeding and could probably use a steri-strip or a couple stiches. She did not want to go home. She loves being at school. First she wanted to know if I had any thread to sew it up. Then when I said it's not the right kind of thread, " Can't you get some and stich it up?" I am not a doctor. Her response whenever I need to set the record straight is, "Oh yeah, that's right!"

I went down to the multiple needs class. Two of the students were at the floor mat. The idea was to do some sit-ups. I got down on the mat and started to do some sit-ups and asked them to join me. The one standing got on the mat next to me and just laughed! The student that was already on the mat, got up and held my feet down so I couldn't cheat!

I was asked in the hallway, if I could fix her loose screw. I kept the giggle to myself. Her glasses needed tightening. The beauty of these glasses was her creativeness. The original frames broke, so she took the lenses out and found these frames at a drugstore. No they weren't the same shape, but they fit snuggly in place and were cute frames! Student MacGyver!
I have had several times I have needed to fix glasses. One student's glasses had a different stem on one side and they didn't even sit square on her head. It was really bugging her. No doubt! Until she got new glasses, I put a paperclip at the end of the stem to weight it and then wrapped medical tape around it. Much better!

We are coming to the last few weeks of the school year. Prom is on Saturday night. One of my "regulars" that comes in to brush his teeth after lunch had things on his mind today. His mouth full of toothpaste, first he tells me he is getting his haircut tomorrow. When I didn't say much, he proceeds to tell me how nervous he is. He tells me prom is Saturday and I don't know how to slow dance. I showed him how simple it is to slow dance, "Move your feet this way, you can slowly move in a circle." He looks at me, spits out his toothpaste and says, "I don't want to look dumb!" I said, " Don't you think you would look better moving on the dance floor, as opposed to just standing there?" To which he replies, "Touché!"

My friend Martha and I have been friends forever. She is totally on board with helping me. She is on a constant quest to collect items for the girls and boys events throughout the year. She wanted to make corsages for the girls for prom this year. I found out the girls get a corsage at the door the night of prom. Two girls in the multiple needs class will not be going to prom. We talked about it. She made two beautiful corsages and dropped them off at school. I gave her a tour of the school and we dropped in on the multiple needs class. They all said hi to Martha and made her feel welcome. Prom is Saturday night; tomorrow the two girls will get their corsages to wear all day at school. I brought each girl down one at a time to my office the next morning. One, I French braided her hair, put on some cologne and gave her the wrist corsage. She was thrilled! The other girl, I put eye shadow on, sprayed on some cologne and put on her wrist corsage. The smile was priceless! They both wore their corsages all day long. I took a picture of each of them. They have a book they are putting pictures in, so that's where they went. A memory.

The students have a class that as part of the curriculum they put together the school yearbook. They take pictures, gather pictures others have taken during the school year and make a CD. Every student gets a copy. Through the course of the year you get your picture taken, whether you like it or not. Grow up; you are the adult! Sure, you can take my picture. I had a student ask if he could take my picture just the other day. He asked a teacher walking by to take the picture. He came over to stand by me and put his arm around me. Appreciation comes in all forms.

Prom was last night. The students always look so nice all dressed up. They like it when staff shows up. Miss "Boogie-Woogie" was ready to dance a little tonight. She even joined the conga line. The student who was afraid he would look dumb on the dance floor? He was lost in the crowd with his date all night. They looked great! The high school that puts this on, I can't say enough about what a great job they do.

Last year there was a student that I became like her second mom. Her family has been through a lot. This gal would be fine one minute and full out sobbing the next. After I got to know her better, I could sometimes get her out of her "funk". One day when she was crying, I looked at her and said,

"Are you friggin' kiddin' me?" She stopped and looked up at me. "That's what I always say!" "I know that's why I said it!" It was done. A smile came over her face and back to business. She is out of our school district, so did not return this past fall. Last week I got a phone call from her. She wanted to know if I was busy next Friday. She wants me to come to her school's prom.

Another one of my life lessons is to never go back on a promise. I promised to come and I did. Steve came with me. He's such a good sport! Three proms in two years! We got hung up at Wal-Mart when we ran into an acquaintance that has the gift of gab. I finally had to say we had to leave; ten minutes later we were through the checkout and heading to the car. We got to the high school about thirty minutes later than I had said. We walked into the gym and she was there waiting with her care attendant. Her face lit up, she ran toward me and about knocked me over to give me a hug. "You are here! You're here!" She had cried twice waiting for me to get there. She introduced me to all her teachers and friends as, "My nurse, Kelly." For her free prom picture, she wanted me to be in it along with her care attendant and a male friend. "I don't like him, but he likes me; he bought me this corsage, I got him a boutonniere; I just need to say hi to him and then he can go home…" Steve being the good sport held all our purses while we had the picture taken. If she wanted to leave my side, she would tell me not to leave,

"You're not going to leave are you?" I was glad I went! It was good to see her and hear she is doing well.

I like to make my own health posters and displays. I found some one-liners that I liked and made a big poster over the toilet in the health office bathroom a couple of months ago. My two favorites are: Flushing the toilet, it is about as easy as pushing a button and You don't have to brush all your teeth, only the ones you want to keep. Staff and students notice the latter one often. Today one of the students that use that bathroom at least twice a day came out and was pointing back toward the bathroom. He's laughing and tells me the poster above the toilet is funny! He asks how long it has been there. When I tell him a couple of months, he just can't believe he never noticed it before today.

I said before that the students don't do well with change. I got my haircut a little different one time and a student told me right away, "Geez, you are wearing your hair different and now I have to get use to it!"

I wear a lab coat every day for several reasons, one of which is to carry the keys to the office and medication cupboard. I was getting too warm and took the jacket off one afternoon. A student noticed it right away. "You are wearing a different shirt." "No, I'm not." "Yes, you are!" "No, I just took my lab jacket off."

We are getting to the time of the year when students are starting to give their graduation presentations. I sat in on one today. She is graduating from the multiple needs class. She did a great job. She smiled the whole time and was so proud of herself. I have done daily care with her for the past two years with the help of one of the Paras. We laugh and tease around a lot with this student. I am really going to miss her.

We all have "catch phrases"; the staff and students are no different than anyone else. You don't even have to see their face to know who's talking. My favorites are: "Ohhhh, REALLY?"

" Oh brother!"

"Just kidding!"

"Well, maybe!"

"I look GOOD!"

"You are crazy, Kelly!"

"You are funny, I am NOT going to argue with you!"

"Easy peasy!"

"Let's rock-n-roll!"

"Come on, man!"

"It's like a goat rodeo!"

And my favorite:

"Toughen up Buttercup!"

It was Nurse's Appreciation Day. I never thought anything of it. We have far too many greeting card inspired holidays. The staff gave me a bouquet of daisies. I thought they were kidding. I was really touched. That was Wednesday. Friday rolls around and a student comes in to tell me "Good Morning!" She just stands there and gets this funny smile on her face. "Did you like the card we made you?" I looked at her puzzled and replied, "What card?" She tells me, "Never mind!" and exits the office. That afternoon, several students were standing outside my office. They told me to close my eyes. "No peeking!" When I open my eyes, several students are standing in my office with a banner and a big beautiful card. The card was made out of poster board that said, "School Nurse Appreciation Day". The card has pretty decorative paper triangles and squares folded over. Inside each paper, staff and students wrote a note to me to fill in the blank " Dear Nurse Kelly, I appreciate you because…" I was so touched. They each came up and gave me a hug. I thought I was going to cry! I love my job and these students. They give me so much.

The banner the students made for me. Yes, that is a blue smurf!

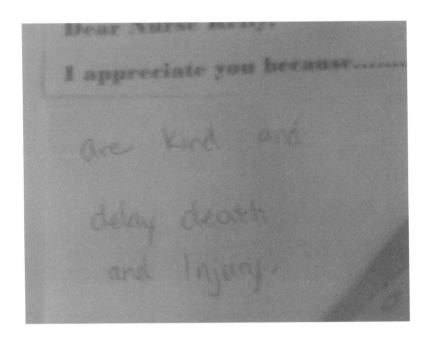

You can't make this stuff up! I laughed so hard; they could probably

hear me down the hall!

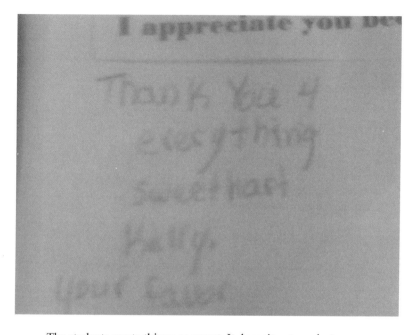

The students wrote things so sweet. It doesn't get any better than that!

One student wanted to write a thank you that would not fit on one of the triangles, so he made his own card. It said, "Dear Kelly, Thank you for healing my wounds from auto dismantling class. Thank you for writing that positive feel good note to me. Thanks also for all the little things you help me with every day. You're the best nurse ever. Thank you."

For all the years I didn't really feel like I made a difference, today I felt like the Grinch who Stole Christmas at the end of the story, my heart grew three sizes larger!

Yesterday the whole school went on an all school field trip to an indoor activity center. They have laser tag, mini golf, arcade games and batting cages. You could feel the testosterone in the air; wait you can smell the sweat in the air! Some of the guys spent a lot of time in those batting cages. The one cage launches baseballs at 65 mph. I watched, as the balls would whiz by their head and wait for it; there was the swing.

Today, I have had a run on visits to the health office for what I call "Batter- Swingitis." "My arm hurts", "It hurts right here!" "It feels like my arms are going to fall off!" My finger-pointing buddy, points to the medication cupboard for his Advil. I asked him, "Do you have Batter-Swingitis, too?" "Yes!"

Over the two years I have known her, she has always called her brother, "My annoying little brother." Apparently he annoys the living daylights out of her. I finally asked her recently if she would tell me what his name actually is. She told me. It's a nice name but she still prefers to call him " My annoying little brother." I imagine when she is 90 years old she will still be calling him that!

The past few Thursdays, one of our classes has been going to the community center. The guys like to shoot hoops. Several of them change in the health office bathroom into shorts and a t-shirt. Two of them were in my office yesterday. As one came out, another one was heading into the bathroom. The second student turns around to see the first one's boxers showing out from his shorts, "Dude, pull up your shorts!" The student explains, "My shorts are too big and I don't have a belt.' The second student tells him to pull the cord on the front of his shorts to tighten them up. He looks down and says, "I thought that cord was just for show!" Just like mom, he adds, "And tuck the extra cord in so it's not hanging out!"

I wash those shorts and t-shirts for several students so they are ready for the next Thursday. One asked very politely if I would wash them for him. "No problem!" He then goes on to give me laundry instructions. I can wash the t-shirt, but don't put it in the dryer. He doesn't like it when the bottom of the shirt turns up. The shirt has holes in it and it isn't as soft when you let it air dry. It doesn't bother me, I just laugh. We all grow up with our little laundry quirks.

Graduation is coming up on Wednesday. We have several students doing their exit presentations and then they come back just for the ceremony. Our student population is dwindling. I am getting that familiar pang. These students are done. I am going to miss them. I am happy to help with the ceremony. It is up close and personal for staff. Last year, I helped them down the steps after they got their diploma so they could go back to their seats. I got to see each student and congratulate him or her. This year I am going to help them to the stage area and keep them at the proper spacing.

It's a dreary rainy day, but despite that, I can still see the bright spots. We had graduation rehearsal at the community college this morning. I just had a student come to see me. She told me she needed my help. I took one look at her eyeglasses and could see what had happened. She explained she just learned how to blow bubbles with bubblegum. Oh my, the bubble went all over and is stuck to both lenses. We started to laugh out loud! She tells me she will never forget this. I used MacGyver tip number 344 and used vegetable oil to get the gum off, washed the lenses with soap and water and then lens cleaner. She is still blowing bubbles as she leaves my office.

A student that has frequented my office over the past two years is graduating. I have called mom and she has called me to touch base. Yesterday, she had a headache. After she had her Tylenol and had rested for 10 minutes, she was ready to go back to class. She looked back at me as she headed out the door, "This will be the last time I come to your office." Today her mom sent her with several boxes of chocolates all wrapped up.

One of them was for me. I said, "Thank you! That was really sweet!" "My mom said it was NESSESSARY!"

Graduation was tonight. I was seated next to "like the son I never had". He was invited to come back and speak to the gradating class. He is nervous, he can't remember his cue to come up on stage, he's afraid the principal will forget to make eye contact with him as a second cue. I tell him to take a deep breath, tell him his verbal cue and make eye contact with the principal and she gives him a "thumbs up" smile. I feel nervous for him, well he is "like the son I never had." He does great. He comes and sits back down beside me. I tell him he did a great job. Now it is my turn to help the students go up to get their diplomas. He asks me if I am nervous. The secretary who has spent weeks putting this together leans across him and asks me if I have the index cards. I teasingly say, "Where are they? I can't find them!" It all goes fine, but he has to say something to me. "Geez, you did a crappy job!" He looks over at her and makes the same comment. I give him a tender punch in the arm for both of us. He laughs and tells me I need to look at his arm. "I am not your school nurse any more; you are fine smarty!" The staff is all so proud of the students and their accomplishments. I am going to miss these students. I got a little attached. Not to worry, there are always new favorites to come and new things that you just can't make up! New ideas and plans are on my mind already for next year.

My buddy likes to draw comic figures. He drew this for me one day when he was sitting in my office before going to a volunteer site. We have a standing joke, just him and me! SNORE!! See, I knew you wouldn't get it.

I stayed after school two weeks in a row to make this mosaic garden stone with the After School Club. I have always enjoyed doing art, crafts and sewing.

After I was given this picture. It seemed strangely familiar to me for some reason. It seemed like I had been photographed like this before.

Oh yeah! It was my senior year of high school in art class.

Some of our students have jobs so they may have a later start to their school day depending on their work schedule. Some days they are just dragging. A couple of times I have been asked for coffee to wake up. I don't have coffee, nor do I drink coffee. Once in a while, I will go to the staff area and pour a bit of coffee in a cup for a student. I did that just the other day. "Thanks, Kelly!" as he walks to class. A staff member saw this and told him, "That was nice of her to do that." His response melted my heart. It was one of those compliments that he didn't know I heard and it was genuine, "Yeah, I know. She loves everyone."

I do love my job and everyone at school. I never thought I would have a job that I enjoyed so much. One of our students summed it up well when speaking to a group of students that will be coming to our school next year, "We are a family here, dysfunctional, but a family!" Touché!